STEAM JUICER COOKBOOK

65 Amazing Juice Recipes

With Beginners Guide, Canning Process and More

Copyright by Betty Walters

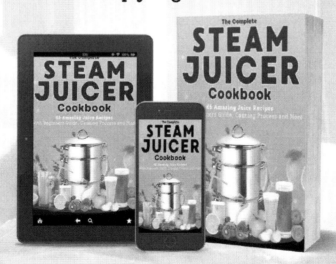

Table of Contents

INTRODUCTION

Growing up, some of my most treasured memories were made in my grandmother's kitchen, where the aroma of simmering fruits and vegetables filled every corner. As she tenderly cared for her beloved steam juicer, its gentle hissing provided the soundtrack to our precious moments together. Gram patiently and carefully extracted every last drop of vibrant, naturally sweet nectar from each batch of perfectly ripe produce.

Those homemade juices, packed with concentrated flavors and nutrients, were more than just drinks; they were liquid memories, evoking the essence of sunny orchards and lush gardens with each sip. Gram's steamy concoctions fueled our bodies and souls, forming the bonds that bind our family traditions.

I can vividly recall perching on a wooden stool, eagerly watching as she transformed piles of ripe strawberries, peaches, and oranges into glistening ruby and amber liquids. The steam juicer's magic captivated me - how could such intense, sun-ripened flavors be so vibrantly captured in liquid form? As I sipped each jewel-toned juice, I was instantly transported to the fields where the fruits were plucked at the peak of perfection.

Vegetable juices were an adventure all their own. Bright greens juices from Gram's bountiful garden regenerated us from the inside out. Her signature cucumber-celery tonic was equally reviving on sultry afternoons as it was restorative during bouts of summer colds.

Years later, as I explored my own culinary interests, that humble steam juicer served as my gateway into the magic of transforming nature's bounty into liquid gold. This cookbook is a love letter to the steaming method, filled with recipes for preserving every season's harvest in delectable juices, concentrates, syrups, jellies and more. May it inspire you to create your own heritage-rich, soulful steam juices to be shared and savored for generations to come.

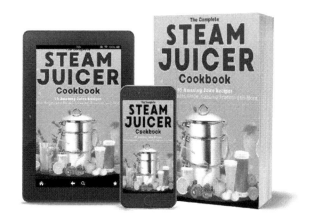

WHAT IS A STEAM JUICER?

A steam juicer is a device used to extract juice from fruits and vegetables using steam as the extraction method. It generates steam that gently cooks the produce, causing the juice to be released and collected in a separate container.

Based On The Information Provided, The Main Parts Of The Stainless-Steel Steam Juicer Are:

Stainless Steel Lid

Top Colander
(put in fruits or vegetables)

Juice Reservoir
(collect dripping juice)

Bottom Pan
(boil water)

2pc Hose Length 16 inch   1pc Clamp

- **Bottom Pot/Base Unit:** This is where water is added and boiled to generate steam.
- **Middle Section/Steam Cone:** The steam rises through this cone-shaped component into the juice kettle and colander.
- **Juice Kettle:** This is the main container that holds the colander filled with produce to be juiced.
- **Colander:** A perforated or mesh basket that sits inside the juice kettle and holds the fruits or vegetables during the juicing process.
- **Silicone Juicing Tube:** A tube attached to the juice kettle allows you to release and collect the extracted juice.
- **Clamp:** A clamp or valve on the silicone juicing tube that you can open or close to control the flow of juice.
- **Large Capacity Stock Pot:** An additional pot included with the steam juicer that can be used for making soups, roasts, or steaming vegetables when combined with the colander.

HOW TO USE A STEAM JUICER

Preparation:
- Wash the fruit and cut large fruits like apples into quarters.
- Remove any potentially poisonous parts like pits, seeds, stems, and leaves.
- Prepare jars, lids, pot holders, and utensils, and have a pitcher of water ready to add to the bottom pan.
- Set up a small table to place the filled jars.

Juicing Process:
- Add water to the bottom pan.
- Place the middle and top pans on the bottom pan, ensuring the silicon tube is hooked to a handle.
- Add the prepared fruit to the top pan.
- Turn on the burner and keep the water boiling.
- When the juice starts rising in the silicon tube, fill the jars. Don't overfill, or juice may overflow through the steam hole into the bottom pan.
- Carefully tip the tube down into a jar and squeeze the metal clamp to release juice. Be cautious, as juice may continue flowing after releasing the clamp. Lift the tube above the juice level in the middle pan to stop the flow.
- Fill jars from the top and cap them immediately.
- Add more fruit to the top pan as it cooks down. Optionally, mash the fruit with a potato masher to extract more juice (may result in more pulp and seeds).

Finishing Up:
- Feed leftover pulp, skins, and seeds to chickens (if available), add to compost, or dispose of them.
- When ready to drink the juice, add water and sweetener to taste.

SOME EXCELLENT ADVANTAGES OF USING A STEAM JUICER

- **High capacity** - the ability to process large batches of up to 10L of fruit at once with minimal labor.
- **Whole fruit can be used** - no need to remove pits/stones from stone fruits beforehand.
- **Simple process** - straightforward operation with little that can go wrong.
- **Pasteurized juice** - the steam extraction pasteurizes the juice for a long shelf life when bottled properly.
- **Energy efficient** - once juiced, no additional electricity is needed to store/preserve it, which is ideal for solar power setups.
- **Versatile uses** - juice can be used for jellies, syrups, sauces, drinks, ice cream bases, enriching kefir, etc.
- **Utilizes overripe fruit** - reduces waste by allowing the use of very ripe fruits.

JUICE CANNING PROCESS

The juice made in a steam juicer is already pasteurized from the steam heating process. However, if you want to store your juice for a longer time, you can further preserve it by canning.

To Can Steam Juiced Juices:
Supplies Needed:

- Canning jars with lids and bands
- Water bath canner or large pot
- Jar lifter
- Canning funnel (optional)

Instructions:

1. Prepare canning jars by washing in hot soapy water and rinsing well. Keep jars hot until ready to fill.
2. Fill your steam juicer and make juice according to regular juicing instructions.
3. Once juice starts flowing, use the tube to fill hot canning jars, leaving 1/4 inch headspace at the top.
4. Use a canning funnel if available to avoid making a mess while filling jars.
5. Wipe rims of filled jars with a damp clean cloth to remove any residue.
6. Place lids on jars and secure bands until fingertip tight.
7. In your water bath canner or large pot, place a rack on the bottom. Add enough water to cover jars by 1-2 inches once added.
8. Using a jar lifter, carefully lower filled jars into the water bath. Make sure they are fully covered.
9. Once all jars are added, cover pot and bring water to a full rolling boil. Process for the time recommended for your elevation:
   - 0-1000 ft: 10 minutes
   - 1001-6000 ft: 15 minutes
   - Above 6000 ft: 20 minutes
10. When processing time is complete, turn off heat and allow to sit for 5 more minutes.
11. Carefully remove hot jars from canner and allow to cool completely on a towel or rack before storing.
12. After 12-24 hours, check seals by pressing on lid. If center is sucked down and doesn't move, it's sealed.

Properly canned and sealed, your steam juicer juices will keep for 12-18 months at cool room temperature. Refrigerate any unsealed jars and use within 1 week.

SOME DISADVANTAGES

- **Nutrient Loss:** The heat involved in steam juicing can degrade heat-sensitive vitamins, minerals, and enzymes compared to cold-press juicing methods. This is an important consideration for those prioritizing maximum nutrient retention.
- **Limited Versatility:** Steam juicers struggle with harder fruits and vegetables like apples, pears, and beets which require more extraction force. They work better on softer produce.
- **Bulky Size:** With multiple components, steam juicers tend to be quite large and take up significant kitchen storage space when not in use.
- **Longer Process:** The steaming method generally takes more time than centrifugal or masticating juicers.
- **Not Ideal for All Produce:** The heat can dull vibrant colors and fresh flavors of certain fruits/vegetables in the finished juice.

Preparation

Pick Ripe Produce: For the best juice yield and flavor, choose ripe fruits and vegetables. Overripe or bruised produce can degrade the flavor and quality of your juice.

Wash and chop: Thoroughly clean your produce to remove dirt and debris. Cut fruits and vegetables into uniform bite-sized pieces. This ensures even steaming and optimal juice extraction.

Water Level: Refer to your juicer's instructions for the proper water level. Too little water can reduce steam production and juice yield, whereas too much water dilutes the juice.

Juicing Process

- **Start with Softer Produce:** Begin with softer fruits and vegetables like berries, tomatoes, or peaches. They steam and release juice more easily. As your experience grows, you can experiment with more firm options.
- **Layering:** Combine fruits and vegetables with varying water content. Place those with more water content on top (like tomatoes) and denser ones below (like apples). This allows for even steaming.
- **Refill Water:** Monitor the juice kettle's water level. If it runs low, refill it with hot water to keep it producing steam.
- **Pulp Management:** You decide how much pulp you want in your juice. Some people enjoy pulp for its fiber content, while others prefer a clearer juice. After collecting the juice, strain it through a fine-mesh sieve or cheesecloth.

Additional Tips

- **Cooling and Storage:** After juicing, store your juice in airtight containers in the refrigerator. Steam-extracted juice may have a shorter shelf life than cold-pressed juice due to heat exposure. For optimal quality, consume within 24-48 hours.
- **Cleaning:** After each use, thoroughly clean your steam juicer with hot, soapy water. Soak any stubborn residue and let all parts dry completely before storing.
- **Experiment with Flavors**: Once you've mastered the fundamentals, try different fruits and vegetables to create unique juice blends. You can also add herbs, spices, or a squeeze of citrus for extra flavor.

1. Classic Apple Juice

Prep Time: 10 minutes / Cook Time: 30 minutes / Serve: 4

Ingredients:

- 8-10 medium-sized apples (any variety you prefer)
- Water

Instructions:

1. Wash the apples thoroughly under running water.
2. Core the apples and cut them into quarters. You can leave the skin on for added flavor and nutrients.
3. Fill the bottom compartment of your steam juicer with water according to the manufacturer's instructions.
4. Place the apple quarters into the top basket of the steam juicer.
5. Assemble the steam juicer and turn on the heat. Allow the apples to steam for about 30 minutes, or until they become soft and pulpy.
6. Once the apples are cooked through, carefully remove the top basket from the steam juicer and let it cool slightly.
7. Transfer the steamed apples to a blender or food processor and blend until smooth.
8. Strain the blended apples through a fine-mesh sieve or cheesecloth to remove any pulp and solids, extracting pure juice.
9. Let the apple juice cool to room temperature before serving. You can refrigerate it for a chilled version.
10. Pour the freshly made apple juice into glasses and enjoy!

2. Tart Cherry Juice

Prep Time: 15 minutes / Cook Time: 30 minutes / Serve: 2

Ingredients:

- 2 cups fresh tart cherries, pitted
- Water
- Honey or sweetener of your choice (optional)

Instructions:

1. Wash the tart cherries under cold water and remove the pits.
2. Place the pitted cherries into the top compartment of the steam juicer.
3. Fill the bottom compartment of the steam juicer with water as per the manufacturer's instructions.
4. Assemble the steam juicer and turn on the heat. Allow the cherries to steam for about 30 minutes.
5. While the cherries are steaming, you can prepare a simple syrup by combining equal parts water and honey in a saucepan. Heat the mixture over medium heat until the honey dissolves completely. Allow the syrup to cool before using.
6. Once steamed, carefully remove the top basket from the steam juicer and let the cherries cool slightly.
7. Transfer the steamed cherries to a blender or food processor and blend until smooth.
8. Strain the blended cherries through a fine-mesh sieve or cheesecloth to remove any pulp and solids, extracting pure juice.
9. Stir in the desired amount of simple syrup or sweetener to taste, if using.
10. Refrigerate the tart cherry juice until chilled.
11. Serve the juice over ice in glasses, garnished with whole cherries or a sprig of mint, if desired. Enjoy the tangy and refreshing flavor of homemade cherry juice!

3. Blueberry-Orange Juice

Prep Time: 10 minutes / Cook Time: 20 minutes / Serve: 2

Ingredients:

- 1 cup fresh blueberries
- Juice of 2 oranges
- Water

Instructions:

1. Place the fresh blueberries into the top compartment of the steam juicer.
2. Squeeze the juice of two oranges over the blueberries.
3. Fill the bottom compartment of the steam juicer with water as per the manufacturer's instructions.
4. Assemble the steam juicer and turn on the heat. Allow the blueberries to steam for about 20 minutes.
5. Once steamed, carefully remove the top basket from the steam juicer and let the blueberries cool slightly.
6. Transfer the steamed blueberries to a blender or food processor and blend until smooth.
7. Strain the blended mixture through a fine-mesh sieve or cheesecloth to remove any pulp and solids, extracting pure juice.
8. Refrigerate the blueberry-orange juice until chilled.
9. Serve the juice over ice in glasses, garnished with a few fresh blueberries or an orange slice, if desired. Enjoy the vibrant burst of flavor in every sip!

4. Zesty Lemonade

Prep Time: 10 minutes / Cook Time: 25 minutes / Serve: 4

Ingredients:

- 4 large lemons
- Water
- Sugar or sweetener of your choice (optional)

Instructions:

1. Wash the lemons thoroughly under cold water.
2. Cut the lemons in half and extract the juice using a citrus juicer or handheld citrus reamer.
3. Pour the freshly squeezed lemon juice into the top compartment of the steam juicer.
4. Fill the bottom compartment of the steam juicer with water according to the manufacturer's instructions.
5. Assemble the steam juicer and turn on the heat. Allow the lemon juice to steam for about 25 minutes.
6. While the lemon juice is steaming, you can prepare a simple syrup by combining equal parts water and sugar in a saucepan. Heat the mixture over medium heat until the sugar dissolves completely. Allow the syrup to cool before using.
7. Once steamed, carefully remove the top basket from the steam juicer and let the lemon juice cool slightly.
8. Transfer the steamed lemon juice to a pitcher and add the desired amount of simple syrup to taste, if using. Stir well to combine.
9. Refrigerate the zesty lemonade until chilled.
10. Serve the lemonade over ice cubes in glasses, garnished with lemon slices or sprigs of fresh mint, if desired. Enjoy your homemade lemonade!

5. Tangy Grapefruit Juice

Prep Time: 5 minutes / Cook Time: 20 minutes / Serve: 2

Ingredients:

- 2 large grapefruits
- Water

Instructions:

1. Rinse the grapefruits thoroughly under cold water.
2. Cut the grapefruits in half and extract the juice using a citrus juicer or a handheld citrus reamer.
3. Pour the freshly squeezed grapefruit juice into the top compartment of the steam juicer.
4. Fill the bottom compartment of the steam juicer with water as per the manufacturer's instructions.
5. Assemble the steam juicer and turn on the heat. Allow the grapefruit juice to steam for about 20 minutes.
6. Once steamed, carefully remove the top basket from the steam juicer and let it cool slightly.
7. Transfer the steamed grapefruit juice to a pitcher and refrigerate until chilled.
8. Stir the juice before serving to distribute any pulp evenly.
9. Pour the tangy grapefruit juice into glasses filled with ice cubes.
10. Garnish with a slice of grapefruit or mint leaves for an extra touch of freshness. Enjoy your refreshing drink!

6. Sweet Strawberry Juice

Prep Time: 15 minutes / Cook Time: 30 minutes / Serve: 2

Ingredients:

- 2 cups fresh strawberries, washed and hulled
- Water
- Sugar or sweetener of your choice (optional)

Instructions:

1. Wash the strawberries under cold water and remove the hulls.
2. Cut the strawberries into halves or quarters, depending on their size.
3. Place the strawberries into the top compartment of the steam juicer.
4. Fill the bottom compartment of the steam juicer with water according to the manufacturer's instructions.
5. Assemble the steam juicer and turn on the heat. Allow the strawberries to steam for about 30 minutes.
6. While the strawberries are steaming, you can prepare a simple syrup by combining equal parts water and sugar in a saucepan. Heat the mixture over medium heat until the sugar dissolves completely. Allow the syrup to cool before using.
7. Once steamed, carefully remove the top basket from the steam juicer and let the strawberries cool slightly.
8. Transfer the steamed strawberries to a blender or food processor and blend until smooth.
9. Strain the blended strawberries through a fine-mesh sieve or cheesecloth to remove any pulp and solids, extracting pure juice.
10. Stir in the desired amount of simple syrup to sweeten the juice, if using. Serve the sweet strawberry juice over ice in glasses, garnished with whole strawberries or mint leaves, if desired. Enjoy your refreshing drink!

7. Refreshing Watermelon Juice

Prep Time: 10 minutes / Cook Time: 20 minutes / Serve: 4

Ingredients:

- 4 cups seedless watermelon, cubed
- Water

Instructions:

1. Cut the seedless watermelon into small cubes, discarding any seeds.
2. Place the watermelon cubes into the top compartment of the steam juicer.
3. Fill the bottom compartment of the steam juicer with water as per the manufacturer's instructions.
4. Assemble the steam juicer and turn on the heat. Allow the watermelon to steam for about 20 minutes.
5. Once steamed, carefully remove the top basket from the steam juicer and let the watermelon cool slightly.
6. Transfer the steamed watermelon to a blender or food processor and blend until smooth.
7. Strain the blended watermelon through a fine-mesh sieve or cheesecloth to remove any pulp and solids, extracting pure juice.
8. Refrigerate the refreshing watermelon juice until chilled.
9. Serve the juice over ice in glasses, garnished with small watermelon wedges or mint leaves, if desired. Enjoy the cool and hydrating taste of summer!

8. Tropical Pineapple-Orange Juice

Prep Time: 10 minutes / Cook Time: 25 minutes / Serve: 4

Ingredients:

- 2 cups fresh pineapple chunks
- 2 large oranges, peeled and segmented
- Water

Instructions:

1. Cut the fresh pineapple into small chunks, discarding the core.
2. Peel the oranges and separate them into segments, removing any seeds.
3. Combine the pineapple chunks and orange segments in the top compartment of the steam juicer.
4. Fill the bottom compartment of the steam juicer with water according to the manufacturer's instructions.
5. Assemble the steam juicer and turn on the heat. Allow the pineapple and oranges to steam for about 25 minutes.
6. Once steamed, carefully remove the top basket from the steam juicer and let the fruit cool slightly.
7. Transfer the steamed pineapple and oranges to a blender or food processor and blend the steamed pineapple and oranges until smooth.
8. Strain the blended mixture through a fine-mesh sieve or cheesecloth to remove any pulp and solids, extracting pure juice.
9. Refrigerate the tropical pineapple-orange juice until chilled.
10. Serve the juice over ice in glasses, garnished with pineapple wedges or orange slices, if desired. Enjoy the refreshing taste of the tropics in every sip!

9. Exotic Mango-Passionfruit Juice

Prep Time: 10 minutes / Cook Time: 25 minutes / Serve: 2

Ingredients:

- 1 large ripe mango, peeled and diced
- Pulp of 4 passion fruits
- Water

Instructions:

1. Peel the ripe mango and cut it into small dice.
2. Cut the passion fruits in half and scoop out the pulp using a spoon.
3. Combine the diced mango and passionfruit pulp in the top compartment of the steam juicer.
4. Fill the bottom compartment of the steam juicer with water according to the manufacturer's instructions.
5. Assemble the steam juicer and turn on the heat. Allow the mango and passionfruit to steam for about 25 minutes.
6. Once steamed, carefully remove the top basket from the steam juicer and let the fruits cool slightly.
7. Transfer the steamed mango and passionfruit to a blender or food processor and blend until smooth.
8. Strain the blended mixture through a fine-mesh sieve or cheesecloth to remove any pulp and solids, extracting pure juice.
9. Refrigerate the exotic mango-passionfruit juice until chilled.
10. Serve the juice over ice in glasses, garnished with mango slices or passionfruit seeds, if desired. Enjoy the tropical burst of flavor in every sip!

10. Cranberry-Pomegranate Elixir

Prep Time: 10 minutes / Cook Time: 30 minutes / Serve: 2

Ingredients:

- 1 cup fresh cranberries
- 1/2 cup pomegranate seeds
- Water
- Honey or sweetener of your choice (optional)

Instructions:

1. Rinse the fresh cranberries under cold water.
2. Deseed the pomegranate and measure out 1/2 cup of seeds.
3. Combine the cranberries and pomegranate seeds in the top compartment of the steam juicer.
4. Fill the bottom compartment of the steam juicer with water as per the manufacturer's instructions.
5. Assemble the steam juicer and turn on the heat. Allow the cranberries and pomegranate seeds to steam for about 30 minutes.
6. While the fruits are steaming, you can prepare a simple syrup by combining equal parts water and honey in a saucepan. Heat the mixture over medium heat until the honey dissolves completely. Allow the syrup to cool before using.
7. Once steamed, carefully remove the top basket from the steam juicer and let the fruits cool slightly.
8. Transfer the steamed cranberries and pomegranate seeds to a blender or food processor and blend until smooth.
9. Strain the blended mixture through a fine-mesh sieve or cheesecloth to remove any pulp and solids, extracting pure juice.
10. Stir in the desired amount of simple syrup or sweetener to taste, if using.
11. Refrigerate the cranberry-pomegranate elixir until chilled.
12. Serve the juice over ice in glasses, garnished with a few cranberries or pomegranate arils, if desired. Enjoy the antioxidant-rich goodness of this vibrant elixir!

11. Peach Nectar

Prep Time: 10 minutes / Cook Time: 25 minutes / Serve: 4

Ingredients:

- 4 ripe peaches, pitted and sliced
- Water

Instructions:

1. Wash the ripe peaches under cold water and remove the pits.
2. Slice the peaches into wedges or chunks.
3. Place the sliced peaches into the top compartment of the steam juicer.
4. Fill the bottom compartment of the steam juicer with water according to the manufacturer's instructions.
5. Assemble the steam juicer and turn on the heat. Allow the peaches to steam for about 25 minutes.
6. Once steamed, carefully remove the top basket from the steam juicer and let the peaches cool slightly.
7. Transfer the steamed peaches to a blender or food processor and blend until smooth.
8. Strain the blended peaches through a fine-mesh sieve or cheesecloth to remove any pulp and solids, extracting pure juice.
9. Refrigerate the peach nectar until chilled.
10. Serve the juice over ice in glasses, garnished with a slice of peach or a sprig of mint, if desired. Enjoy the sweet and fragrant taste of homemade peach nectar!

12. Ginger-Lime Pear Juice

Prep Time: 10 minutes / Cook Time: 25 minutes / Serve: 2

Ingredients:

- 2 ripe pears, peeled and sliced
- 1-inch piece of fresh ginger, peeled and thinly sliced
- Juice of 1 lime
- Water

Instructions:

1. Place the sliced pears and ginger slices into the top compartment of the steam juicer.
2. Squeeze the juice of one lime over the pear and ginger mixture.
3. Fill the bottom compartment of the steam juicer with water according to the manufacturer's instructions.
4. Assemble the steam juicer and turn on the heat. Allow the pears and ginger to steam for about 25 minutes.
5. Once steamed, carefully remove the top basket from the steam juicer and let the mixture cool slightly.
6. Transfer the steamed pears and ginger to a blender or food processor and blend until smooth.
7. Strain the blended mixture through a fine-mesh sieve or cheesecloth to remove any pulp and solids, extracting pure juice.
8. Refrigerate the ginger-lime pear juice until chilled.
9. Serve the juice over ice in glasses, garnished with a lime slice or a sprig of mint, if desired. Enjoy the unique flavor combination of ginger, lime, and pear!

13. Apricot-Mango Splash

Prep Time: 10 minutes / Cook Time: 25 minutes / Serve: 2

Ingredients:

- 1 ripe mango, peeled and diced
- 2 ripe apricots, pitted and sliced
- Water

Instructions:

1. Place the diced mango and sliced apricots into the top compartment of the steam juicer.
2. Fill the bottom compartment of the steam juicer with water as per the manufacturer's instructions.
3. Assemble the steam juicer and turn on the heat. Allow the mango and apricots to steam for about 25 minutes.
4. Once steamed, carefully remove the top basket from the steam juicer and let the fruits cool slightly.
5. Transfer the steamed mango and apricots to a blender or food processor and blend until smooth.
6. Strain the blended mixture through a fine-mesh sieve or cheesecloth to remove any pulp and solids, extracting pure juice.
7. Refrigerate the apricot-mango splash until chilled.
8. Serve the juice over ice in glasses, garnished with a slice of mango or a few apricot slices, if desired. Enjoy the refreshing burst of apricot and mango flavors!

14. Passionfruit-Mango Juice

Prep Time: 10 minutes / Cook Time: 25 minutes / Serve: 2

Ingredients:

- Pulp of 3 passion fruits
- 1 ripe mango, peeled and diced
- Water

Instructions:

1. Scoop out the pulp of three passion fruits and place it into the top compartment of the steam juicer.
2. Peel the ripe mango and cut it into small dice.
3. Add the diced mango to the passionfruit pulp in the steam juicer.
4. Fill the bottom compartment of the steam juicer with water according to the manufacturer's instructions.
5. Assemble the steam juicer and turn on the heat. Allow the passionfruit and mango to steam for about 25 minutes.
6. Once steamed, carefully remove the top basket from the steam juicer and let the fruits cool slightly.
7. Transfer the steamed passionfruit and mango to a blender or food processor and blend until smooth.
8. Strain the blended mixture through a fine-mesh sieve or cheesecloth to remove any pulp and solids, extracting pure juice.
9. Refrigerate the passionfruit-mango juice until chilled.
10. Serve the juice over ice in glasses, garnished with a slice of mango or a passionfruit seed, if desired. Enjoy the tropical paradise in a glass!

15. Blackberry-Lemonade

Prep Time: 10 minutes / Cook Time: 20 minutes / Serve: 2

Ingredients:

- 1 cup fresh blackberries
- Juice of 2 lemons
- Water
- Sugar or sweetener of your choice (optional)

Instructions:

1. Place the fresh blackberries into the top compartment of the steam juicer.
2. Squeeze the juice of two lemons over the blackberries.
3. Fill the bottom compartment of the steam juicer with water as per the manufacturer's instructions.
4. Assemble the steam juicer and turn on the heat. Allow the blackberries to steam for about 20 minutes.
5. Once steamed, carefully remove the top basket from the steam juicer and let the blackberries cool slightly.
6. Transfer the steamed blackberries to a blender or food processor and blend until smooth.
7. Strain the blended mixture through a fine-mesh sieve or cheesecloth to remove any pulp and solids, extracting pure juice.
8. If desired, sweeten the juice with sugar or sweetener to taste, stirring until dissolved.
9. Refrigerate the blackberry-lemonade until chilled.
10. Serve the juice over ice in glasses, garnished with a lemon slice or a few whole blackberries, if desired. Enjoy the refreshing and tangy flavor of homemade blackberry-lemonade!

16. Mixed Berry Blast

Prep Time: 10 minutes / Cook Time: 25 minutes / Serve: 2

Ingredients:

- 1/2 cup fresh strawberries, hulled and halved
- 1/2 cup fresh raspberries
- 1/2 cup fresh blueberries
- Water
- Honey or sweetener of your choice (optional)

Instructions:

1. Combine the fresh strawberries, raspberries, and blueberries in the top compartment of the steam juicer.
2. Fill the bottom compartment of the steam juicer with water according to the manufacturer's instructions.
3. Assemble the steam juicer and turn on the heat. Allow the mixed berries to steam for about 25 minutes.
4. Once steamed, carefully remove the top basket from the steam juicer and let the berries cool slightly.
5. Transfer the steamed mixed berries to a blender or food processor and blend until smooth.
6. Strain the blended mixture through a fine-mesh sieve or cheesecloth to remove any pulp and solids, extracting pure juice.
7. If desired, sweeten the juice with honey or sweetener to taste, stirring until dissolved.
8. Refrigerate the mixed berry blast until chilled.
9. Serve the juice over ice in glasses, garnished with a few whole berries or a sprig of mint, if desired. Enjoy the burst of berry goodness in every sip!

17. Pineapple-Coconut Refresher

Prep Time: 10 minutes / Cook Time: 25 minutes / Serve: 2

Ingredients:

- 1 cup fresh pineapple chunks
- 1/2 cup coconut water
- Water

Instructions:

1. Place the fresh pineapple chunks into the top compartment of the steam juicer.
2. Pour the coconut water over the pineapple chunks.
3. Fill the bottom compartment of the steam juicer with water as per the manufacturer's instructions.
4. Assemble the steam juicer and turn on the heat. Allow the pineapple to steam for about 25 minutes.
5. Once steamed, carefully remove the top basket from the steam juicer and let the pineapple cool slightly.
6. Transfer the steamed pineapple to a blender or food processor and blend until smooth.
7. Strain the blended mixture through a fine-mesh sieve or cheesecloth to remove any pulp and solids, extracting pure juice.
8. If desired, add more coconut water to adjust the consistency or sweetness of the juice.
9. Refrigerate the pineapple-coconut refresher until chilled.
10. Serve the juice over ice in glasses, garnished with a pineapple wedge or a sprinkle of shredded coconut, if desired. Enjoy the tropical fusion of pineapple and coconut flavors!

18. Raspberry-Lemonade

Prep Time: 10 minutes / Cook Time: 20 minutes / Serve: 2

Ingredients:

- 1 cup fresh raspberries
- Juice of 2 lemons
- Water
- Sugar or sweetener of your choice (optional)

Instructions:

1. Place the fresh raspberries into the top compartment of the steam juicer.
2. Squeeze the juice of two lemons over the raspberries.
3. Fill the bottom compartment of the steam juicer with water as per the manufacturer's instructions.
4. Assemble the steam juicer and turn on the heat. Allow the raspberries to steam for about 20 minutes.
5. Once steamed, carefully remove the top basket from the steam juicer and let the raspberries cool slightly.
6. Transfer the steamed raspberries to a blender or food processor and blend until smooth.
7. Strain the blended mixture through a fine-mesh sieve or cheesecloth to remove any pulp and solids, extracting pure juice.
8. If desired, sweeten the juice with sugar or sweetener to taste, stirring until dissolved.
9. Refrigerate the raspberry-lemonade until chilled.
10. Serve the juice over ice in glasses, garnished with a lemon slice or a few fresh raspberries, if desired. Enjoy the delightful combination of tart raspberries and zesty lemonade!

19. Kiwi-Strawberry Refresher

Prep Time: 10 minutes / Cook Time: 25 minutes / Serve: 2

Ingredients:

- 2 ripe kiwis, peeled and sliced
- 1 cup fresh strawberries, hulled and halved
- Water

Instructions:

1. Place the sliced kiwis and halved strawberries into the top compartment of the steam juicer.
2. Fill the bottom compartment of the steam juicer with water according to the manufacturer's instructions.
3. Assemble the steam juicer and turn on the heat. Allow the kiwis and strawberries to steam for about 25 minutes.
4. Once steamed, carefully remove the top basket from the steam juicer and let the fruits cool slightly.
5. Transfer the steamed kiwis and strawberries to a blender or food processor and blend until smooth.
6. Strain the blended mixture through a fine-mesh sieve or cheesecloth to remove any pulp and solids, extracting pure juice.
7. Refrigerate the kiwi-strawberry refresher until chilled.
8. Serve the juice over ice in glasses, garnished with a kiwi slice or a strawberry half, if desired. Enjoy the vibrant combination of kiwi and strawberry flavors!

20. Pear-Ginger Elixir

Prep Time: 10 minutes / Cook Time: 25 minutes / Serve: 2

Ingredients:

- 2 ripe pears, peeled and sliced
- 1-inch piece of fresh ginger, peeled and thinly sliced
- Water

Instructions:

1. Place the sliced pears and ginger slices into the top compartment of the steam juicer.
2. Fill the bottom compartment of the steam juicer with water according to the manufacturer's instructions.
3. Assemble the steam juicer and turn on the heat. Allow the pears and ginger to steam for about 25 minutes.
4. Once steamed, carefully remove the top basket from the steam juicer and let the mixture cool slightly.
5. Transfer the steamed pears and ginger to a blender or food processor and blend until smooth.
6. Strain the blended mixture through a fine-mesh sieve or cheesecloth to remove any pulp and solids, extracting pure juice.
7. Refrigerate the pear-ginger elixir until chilled.
8. Serve the juice over ice in glasses, garnished with a slice of pear or a twist of ginger, if desired. Enjoy the invigorating combination of pear and ginger flavors!

21. Melon Medley Juice

Prep Time: 10 minutes / Cook Time: 20 minutes / Serve: 2

Ingredients:

- 1 cup cubed watermelon
- 1 cup cubed cantaloupe
- 1 cup cubed honeydew melon
- Water

Instructions:

1. Place the cubed watermelon, cantaloupe, and honeydew melon into the top compartment of the steam juicer.
2. Fill the bottom compartment of the steam juicer with water according to the manufacturer's instructions.
3. Assemble the steam juicer and turn on the heat. Allow the melons to steam for about 20 minutes.
4. Once steamed, carefully remove the top basket from the steam juicer and let the melons cool slightly.
5. Transfer the steamed melons to a blender or food processor and blend until smooth.
6. Strain the blended mixture through a fine-mesh sieve or cheesecloth to remove any pulp and solids, extracting pure juice.
7. Refrigerate the melon medley juice until chilled.
8. Serve the juice over ice in glasses, garnished with a small melon ball or a mint leaf, if desired. Enjoy the refreshing blend of sweet and juicy melons!

22. Plum-Berry Elixir

Prep Time: 10 minutes / Cook Time: 25 minutes / Serve: 2

Ingredients:

- 2 ripe plums, pitted and sliced
- 1/2 cup fresh blackberries
- 1/2 cup fresh raspberries
- Water

Instructions:

1. Place the sliced plums, blackberries, and raspberries into the top compartment of the steam juicer.
2. Fill the bottom compartment of the steam juicer with water as per the manufacturer's instructions.
3. Assemble the steam juicer and turn on the heat. Allow the fruits to steam for about 25 minutes.
4. Once steamed, carefully remove the top basket from the steam juicer and let the fruits cool slightly.
5. Transfer the steamed fruits to a blender or food processor and blend until smooth.
6. Strain the blended mixture through a fine-mesh sieve or cheesecloth to remove any pulp and solids, extracting pure juice.
7. Refrigerate the plum-berry elixir until chilled.
8. Serve the juice over ice in glasses, garnished with a plum slice or a few berries, if desired. Enjoy the delightful combination of plum and berry flavors!

23. Apple-Pomegranate Refresher

Prep Time: 10 minutes / Cook Time: 30 minutes / Serve: 2

Ingredients:
- 2 medium apples, cored and sliced
- Seeds of 1 pomegranate
- Water

Instructions:
1. Place the sliced apples and pomegranate seeds into the top compartment of the steam juicer.
2. Fill the bottom compartment of the steam juicer with water according to the manufacturer's instructions.
3. Assemble the steam juicer and turn on the heat. Allow the apples and pomegranate seeds to steam for about 30 minutes.
4. Once steamed, carefully remove the top basket from the steam juicer and let the fruits cool slightly.
5. Transfer the steamed apples and pomegranate seeds to a blender or food processor and blend until smooth.
6. Strain the blended mixture through a fine-mesh sieve or cheesecloth to remove any pulp and solids, extracting pure juice.
7. Refrigerate the apple-pomegranate refresher until chilled.
8. Serve the juice over ice in glasses, garnished with a slice of apple or a sprinkle of pomegranate seeds, if desired. Enjoy the crisp apple flavor combined with the tartness of pomegranate!

24. Banana-Berry Smoothie

Prep Time: 10 minutes / Cook Time: 10 minutes / Serve: 2

Ingredients:
- 1 ripe banana
- 1/2 cup fresh strawberries
- 1/2 cup fresh blueberries
- 1/2 cup fresh raspberries
- Water

Instructions:
1. Peel the ripe banana and break it into chunks.
2. Place the banana chunks, strawberries, blueberries, and raspberries into the top compartment of the steam juicer.
3. Fill the bottom compartment of the steam juicer with water according to the manufacturer's instructions.
4. Assemble the steam juicer and turn on the heat. Allow the fruits to steam for about 10 minutes.
5. Once steamed, carefully remove the top basket from the steam juicer and let the fruits cool slightly.
6. Transfer the steamed fruits to a blender or food processor and blend until smooth.
7. For a thinner consistency, you can add water or milk to the smoothie.
8. Serve the banana-berry smoothie immediately in glasses, garnished with a few whole berries or a slice of banana, if desired. Enjoy the creamy and fruity goodness of this refreshing smoothie!

25. Cucumber-Mint Cooler

Prep Time: 10 minutes / Cook Time: 10 minutes / Serve: 2

Ingredients:
- 1 large cucumber, peeled and sliced
- Handful of fresh mint leaves
- Water

Instructions:
1. Place the sliced cucumber and fresh mint leaves into the top compartment of the steam juicer.
2. Fill the bottom compartment of the steam juicer with water according to the manufacturer's instructions.
3. Assemble the steam juicer and turn on the heat. Allow the cucumber and mint to steam for about 10 minutes.
4. Once steamed, carefully remove the top basket from the steam juicer and let the cucumber and mint cool slightly.
5. Transfer the steamed cucumber and mint to a blender or food processor and blend until smooth.
6. Strain the blended mixture through a fine-mesh sieve or cheesecloth to remove any pulp and solids, extracting pure juice.
7. Refrigerate the cucumber-mint cooler until chilled.
8. Serve the juice over ice in glasses, garnished with a sprig of fresh mint or a cucumber slice, if desired. Enjoy the crisp and refreshing taste of cucumber paired with the coolness of mint!

26. Pear-Apple-Ginger Elixir

Prep Time: 10 minutes / Cook Time: 25 minutes / Serve: 2

Ingredients:

- 1 ripe pear, peeled and sliced
- 1 medium apple, cored and sliced
- 1-inch piece of fresh ginger, peeled and thinly sliced
- Water

Instructions:

1. Place the sliced pear, apple, and ginger slices into the top compartment of the steam juicer.
2. Fill the bottom compartment of the steam juicer with water according to the manufacturer's instructions.
3. Assemble the steam juicer and turn on the heat. Allow the fruits and ginger to steam for about 25 minutes.
4. Once steamed, carefully remove the top basket from the steam juicer and let the mixture cool slightly.
5. Transfer the steamed fruits and ginger to a blender or food processor and blend until smooth.
6. Strain the blended mixture through a fine-mesh sieve or cheesecloth to remove any pulp and solids, extracting pure juice.
7. Refrigerate the pear-apple-ginger elixir until chilled.
8. Serve the juice over ice in glasses, garnished with a slice of pear or a twist of ginger, if desired. Enjoy the harmonious blend of pear, apple, and ginger flavors!

VEGETABLE JUICES

27. Carrot-Orange Zinger

Prep Time: 10 minutes / Cook Time: 30 minutes / Serve: 2

Ingredients:

- 4 large carrots, peeled and chopped
- Juice of 3 oranges
- 1-inch piece of ginger, peeled and chopped

Instructions:

1. Wash and peel the carrots, then chop them into smaller pieces.
2. Juice the oranges to extract fresh orange juice.
3. Peel and chop the ginger.
4. Place the chopped carrots and ginger into the top compartment of the steam juicer.
5. Fill the bottom compartment of the steam juicer with water according to the manufacturer's instructions.
6. Assemble the steam juicer and turn on the heat. Allow the carrots and ginger to steam for about 30 minutes until they become soft.
7. Once steamed, carefully remove the top basket from the steam juicer and let the carrots and ginger cool slightly.
8. Transfer the steamed carrots and ginger to a blender or food processor.
9. Add the freshly squeezed orange juice to the blender.
10. Blend the mixture until smooth.
11. Pour the juice into serving glasses and serve immediately. Enjoy the zesty and invigorating flavor of carrot-orange zinger!

28. Beet-Apple Energizer

Prep Time: 10 minutes / Cook Time: 30 minutes / Serve: 2

Ingredients:
- 2 medium-sized beets, peeled and chopped
- 2 apples, cored and chopped
- Juice of 1 lemon

Instructions:
1. Wash and peel the beets, then chop them into smaller pieces.
2. Core and chop the apples.
3. Juice the lemon.
4. Place the chopped beets into the top compartment of the steam juicer.
5. Fill the bottom compartment of the steam juicer with water as per the manufacturer's instructions.
6. Assemble the steam juicer and turn on the heat. Allow the beets to steam for about 30 minutes until they become tender.
7. Once steamed, carefully remove the top basket from the steam juicer and let the beets cool slightly.
8. Transfer the steamed beets to a blender or food processor.
9. Add the chopped apples and lemon juice to the blender.
10. Blend the mixture until smooth.
11. Pour the juice into serving glasses and serve immediately. Enjoy the energizing and nutrient-rich beet-apple juice!

29. Tomato-Basil Garden Blend

Prep Time: 10 minutes / Cook Time: 30 minutes / Serve: 2

Ingredients:
- 4 ripe tomatoes, chopped
- Handful of fresh basil leaves
- 1/2 teaspoon salt
- Pinch of black pepper

Instructions:
1. Wash the tomatoes and chop them into smaller pieces.
2. Wash the basil leaves and pat them dry.
3. Place the chopped tomatoes and basil leaves into the top compartment of the steam juicer.
4. Fill the bottom compartment of the steam juicer with water according to the manufacturer's instructions.
5. Assemble the steam juicer and turn on the heat. Allow the tomatoes and basil to steam for about 30 minutes until they become soft.
6. Once steamed, carefully remove the top basket from the steam juicer and let the tomatoes and basil cool slightly.
7. Transfer the steamed tomatoes and basil to a blender or food processor.
8. Add salt and black pepper to the blender.
9. Blend the mixture until smooth.
10. Pour the juice into serving glasses and serve immediately. Enjoy the savory and aromatic tomato-basil garden blend!

30. Cucumber-Mint Refresher

Prep Time: 10 minutes / Cook Time: 30 minutes / Serve: 2

Ingredients:

- 1 large cucumber, chopped
- Handful of fresh mint leaves
- Juice of 1 lime

Instructions:

1. Wash and peel the cucumber, then chop it into smaller pieces.
2. Wash the mint leaves and pat them dry.
3. Place the chopped cucumber and mint leaves into the top compartment of the steam juicer.
4. Fill the bottom compartment of the steam juicer with water according to the manufacturer's instructions.
5. Assemble the steam juicer and turn on the heat. Allow the cucumber and mint to steam for about 30 minutes until they become soft.
6. Once steamed, carefully remove the top basket from the steam juicer and let the cucumber and mint cool slightly.
7. Transfer the steamed cucumber and mint to a blender or food processor.
8. Squeeze the lime juice into the blender.
9. Blend the mixture until smooth.
10. Pour the juice into serving glasses and serve immediately. Enjoy the refreshing and cooling cucumber-mint refresher!

31. Spinach-Kale Power Punch

Prep Time: 10 minutes / Cook Time: 30 minutes / Serve: 2

Ingredients:

- 2 cups fresh spinach leaves
- 1 cup kale leaves, stems removed
- 1 green apple, chopped
- Juice of 1/2 lemon

Instructions:

1. Wash the spinach and kale leaves thoroughly.
2. Core and chop the green apple.
3. Place the spinach, kale, and chopped apple into the top compartment of the steam juicer.
4. Fill the bottom compartment of the steam juicer with water as per the manufacturer's instructions.
5. Assemble the steam juicer and turn on the heat. Allow the spinach, kale, and apple to steam for about 30 minutes until they become tender.
6. Once steamed, carefully remove the top basket from the steam juicer and let the greens and apple cool slightly.
7. Transfer the steamed spinach, kale, and apple to a blender or food processor.
8. Squeeze the lemon juice into the blender.
9. Blend the mixture until smooth.
10. Pour the juice into serving glasses and serve immediately. Enjoy the nutrient-packed spinach-kale power punch!

32. Celery-Cucumber Cooler

Prep Time: 10 minutes / Cook Time: 30 minutes / Serve: 2

Ingredients:

- 4 celery stalks, chopped
- 1 large cucumber
- Juice of 1 lemon
- Handful of fresh parsley leaves

Instructions:

1. Wash the celery stalks and chop them into smaller pieces.
2. Wash and peel the cucumber, then chop it into chunks.
3. Place the chopped celery and cucumber into the top compartment of the steam juicer.
4. Fill the bottom compartment of the steam juicer with water according to the manufacturer's instructions.
5. Assemble the steam juicer and turn on the heat. Allow the celery and cucumber to steam for about 30 minutes until they become tender.
6. Once steamed, carefully remove the top basket from the steam juicer and let the celery and cucumber cool slightly.
7. Transfer the steamed celery and cucumber to a blender or food processor.
8. Squeeze the lemon juice into the blender.
9. Add the fresh parsley leaves to the blender.
10. Blend the mixture until smooth.
11. Pour the juice into serving glasses and serve immediately. Enjoy the crisp and hydrating celery-cucumber cooler!

33. Bell Pepper-Carrot Elixir

Prep Time: 10 minutes / Cook Time: 30 minutes / Serve: 2

Ingredients:

- 2 bell peppers (any color), seeded and chopped
- 2 large carrots, peeled and chopped
- Juice of 1 orange

Instructions:

1. Wash and chop the bell peppers, removing the seeds.
2. Peel and chop the carrots into smaller pieces.
3. Juice the orange to extract fresh orange juice.
4. Place the chopped bell peppers and carrots into the top compartment of the steam juicer.
5. Fill the bottom compartment of the steam juicer with water as per the manufacturer's instructions.
6. Assemble the steam juicer and turn on the heat. Allow the bell peppers and carrots to steam for about 30 minutes until they become tender.
7. Once steamed, carefully remove the top basket from the steam juicer and let the bell peppers and carrots cool slightly.
8. Transfer the steamed bell peppers and carrots to a blender or food processor.
9. Add the freshly squeezed orange juice to the blender.
10. Blend the mixture until smooth.
11. Pour the juice into serving glasses and serve immediately. Enjoy the vibrant and flavorful bell pepper-carrot elixir!

34. Sweet Potato-Ginger Elixir

Prep Time: 10 minutes / Cook Time: 30 minutes / Serve: 2

Ingredients:
- 1 large sweet potato, peeled and chopped
- 1-inch piece of fresh ginger, peeled and chopped
- Juice of 1/2 lemon

Instructions:
1. Wash and peel the sweet potato, then chop it into smaller pieces.
2. Peel and chop the ginger.
3. Juice the lemon.
4. Place the chopped sweet potato and ginger into the top compartment of the steam juicer.
5. Fill the bottom compartment of the steam juicer with water according to the manufacturer's instructions.
6. Assemble the steam juicer and turn on the heat. Allow the sweet potato and ginger to steam for about 30 minutes until they become tender.
7. Once steamed, carefully remove the top basket from the steam juicer and let the sweet potato and ginger cool slightly.
8. Transfer the steamed sweet potato and ginger to a blender or food processor.
9. Add the freshly squeezed lemon juice to the blender.
10. Blend the mixture until smooth.
11. Pour the juice into serving glasses and serve immediately. Enjoy the comforting and soothing sweet potato-ginger elixir!

35. Broccoli-Cauliflower Cleanse

Prep Time: 10 minutes / Cook Time: 30 minutes / Serve: 2

Ingredients:
- 1 cup broccoli florets
- 1 cup cauliflower florets
- Juice of 1/2 lemon
- Pinch of cayenne pepper (optional)

Instructions:
1. Wash the broccoli and cauliflower florets thoroughly.
2. Place the florets into the top compartment of the steam juicer.
3. Fill the bottom compartment of the steam juicer with water as per the manufacturer's instructions.
4. Assemble the steam juicer and turn on the heat. Allow the broccoli and cauliflower to steam for about 30 minutes until they become tender.
5. Once steamed, carefully remove the top basket from the steam juicer and let the broccoli and cauliflower cool slightly.
6. Transfer the steamed broccoli and cauliflower to a blender or food processor.
7. Squeeze the lemon juice into the blender.
8. Add a pinch of cayenne pepper if desired for added spice.
9. Blend the mixture until smooth.
10. Pour the juice into serving glasses and serve immediately. Enjoy the detoxifying and cleansing properties of broccoli-cauliflower cleanse!

36. Zucchini-Carrot Cleanser

Prep Time: 10 minutes / Cook Time: 30 minutes / Serve: 2

Ingredients:
- 1 large zucchini, chopped
- 2 large carrots, peeled and chopped
- Juice of 1/2 lemon
- Handful of fresh cilantro leaves

Instructions:
1. Wash and chop the zucchini into smaller pieces.
2. Peel and chop the carrots.
3. Place the chopped zucchini and carrots into the top compartment of the steam juicer.
4. Fill the bottom compartment of the steam juicer with water according to the manufacturer's instructions.
5. Assemble the steam juicer and turn on the heat. Allow the zucchini and carrots to steam for about 30 minutes until they become tender.
6. Once steamed, carefully remove the top basket from the steam juicer and let the zucchini and carrots cool slightly.
7. Transfer the steamed zucchini and carrots to a blender or food processor.
8. Squeeze the lemon juice into the blender.
9. Add the fresh cilantro leaves to the blender.
10. Blend the mixture until smooth.
11. Pour the juice into serving glasses and serve immediately. Enjoy the refreshing and detoxifying zucchini-carrot cleanser!

37. Lemon-Cucumber Spa Water

Prep Time: 5 minutes / Cook Time: 0 minutes / Serve: 2

Ingredients:
- 1 lemon, thinly sliced
- 1/2 cucumber, thinly sliced
- Handful of fresh mint leaves
- Water (filtered or sparkling)
- Ice cubes (optional)

Instructions:
1. Wash the lemon and cucumber thoroughly.
2. Slice the lemon and cucumber into thin rounds.
3. Tear the mint leaves gently to release their aroma.
4. In a large pitcher, combine the lemon slices, cucumber slices, and torn mint leaves.
5. Fill the pitcher with filtered or sparkling water.
6. If desired, add ice cubes to chill the spa water.
7. Stir well to combine the ingredients.
8. Let the spa water sit in the refrigerator for at least 30 minutes to allow the flavors to infuse.
9. Serve the lemon-cucumber spa water chilled over ice, if desired. Enjoy the refreshing and revitalizing taste of this spa-inspired beverage!

38. Minty Watermelon Refresher

Prep Time: 10 minutes / Cook Time: 0 minutes / Serve: 2

Ingredients:

- 2 cups diced watermelon, seeds removed
- Juice of 1 lime
- Handful of fresh mint leaves
- Water
- Ice cubes (optional)

Instructions:

1. Cut the watermelon into small cubes, removing any seeds.
2. Juice the lime to extract fresh lime juice.
3. Wash the mint leaves and pat them dry.
4. In a blender, combine the diced watermelon, lime juice, and mint leaves.
5. Add a splash of water to help with blending.
6. Blend the mixture until smooth.
7. If desired, pour the watermelon mixture through a fine-mesh sieve to remove any pulp.
8. Transfer the watermelon juice to a pitcher.
9. Fill the pitcher with additional water to dilute the juice, adjusting to your taste preference.
10. If desired, add ice cubes to chill the refresher.
11. Stir well and serve the minty watermelon refresher in glasses over ice. Enjoy the cooling and hydrating sensation of this summery drink!

39. Strawberry-Basil Infusion

Prep Time: 10 minutes / Cook Time: 0 minutes / Serve: 2

Ingredients:

- 1 cup fresh strawberries, hulled and sliced
- Handful of fresh basil leaves
- Water
- Ice cubes (optional)

Instructions:

1. Wash the strawberries and remove the stems. Slice them thinly.
2. Wash the basil leaves and pat them dry.
3. In a pitcher, combine the sliced strawberries and basil leaves.
4. Fill the pitcher with water.
5. If desired, add ice cubes to the pitcher to chill the infusion.
6. Stir gently to combine the ingredients.
7. Let the strawberry-basil infusion sit in the refrigerator for at least 1 hour to allow the flavors to meld.
8. Serve the infusion in glasses over ice, if desired. Enjoy the delightful combination of sweet strawberries and aromatic basil in this refreshing drink!

40. Blueberry-Lavender Elixir

Prep Time: 10 minutes / Cook Time: 0 minutes / Serve: 2

Ingredients:

- 1 cup fresh blueberries
- 1 tablespoon dried lavender buds
- Honey or agave syrup (optional)
- Water
- Ice cubes (optional)

Instructions:

1. Rinse the fresh blueberries under cold water and drain them.
2. In a teapot or heatproof pitcher, place the dried lavender buds.
3. Boil water and pour it over the lavender buds.
4. Allow the lavender to steep in the hot water for about 5 minutes to infuse.
5. Strain the lavender-infused water to remove the buds, then let it cool to room temperature.
6. In a blender, combine the fresh blueberries and cooled lavender-infused water.
7. Blend the mixture until smooth.
8. If desired, sweeten the elixir with honey or agave syrup to taste, blending again to combine.
9. Pour the blueberry-lavender elixir into serving glasses over ice cubes, if desired.
10. Garnish with a sprig of fresh lavender or a few whole blueberries for an extra touch. Enjoy the delicate floral notes and antioxidant-rich goodness of this elixir!

41. Ginger-Peach Iced Tea

Prep Time: 10 minutes / Cook Time: 10 minutes / Serve: 4

Ingredients:

- 4 ripe peaches, pitted and sliced
- 1/4 cup fresh ginger, sliced
- 4 cups water
- 4 black tea bags
- Honey or sugar (optional)
- Ice cubes
- Fresh mint leaves for garnish (optional)

Instructions:

1. In a large saucepan, combine the sliced peaches, sliced ginger, and water.
2. Bring the mixture to a boil over medium-high heat.
3. Once boiling, reduce the heat to low and let the mixture simmer for about 5 minutes to infuse the flavors.
4. Remove the saucepan from the heat and add the black tea bags.
5. Let the tea bags steep in the peach-ginger mixture for about 5 minutes to brew.
6. After steeping, remove the tea bags and discard them.
7. If desired, sweeten the iced tea with honey or sugar to taste, stirring until dissolved.
8. Allow the peach-ginger iced tea to cool to room temperature, then refrigerate until chilled.
9. To serve, fill glasses with ice cubes and pour the chilled tea over the ice.
10. Garnish each glass with fresh mint leaves, if desired. Enjoy the refreshing and aromatic flavor of ginger-peach iced tea on a hot day!

42. Hibiscus-Rosehip Cooler

Prep Time: 5 minutes / Cook Time: 5 minutes / Serve: 4

Ingredients:

- 4 hibiscus tea bags
- 2 tablespoons dried rosehips
- 4 cups water
- Honey or agave syrup (optional)
- Ice cubes
- Fresh lemon slices for garnish (optional)

Instructions:

1. In a medium saucepan, combine the hibiscus tea bags, dried rosehips, and water.
2. Bring the mixture to a boil over medium-high heat.
3. Once boiling, reduce the heat to low and let the mixture simmer for about 5 minutes to infuse the flavors.
4. Remove the saucepan from the heat and discard the tea bags.
5. If desired, sweeten the cooler with honey or agave syrup to taste, stirring until dissolved.
6. Allow the hibiscus-rosehip cooler to cool to room temperature.
7. Once cooled, transfer the mixture to a pitcher and refrigerate until chilled.
8. When ready to serve, fill glasses with ice cubes.
9. Pour the chilled hibiscus-rosehip cooler into the glasses.
10. Garnish each glass with a slice of fresh lemon, if desired.
11. Stir well before sipping to combine the flavors. Enjoy the tart and refreshing taste of this floral-infused cooler!

43. Lavender-Lemon Balm Elixir

Prep Time: 5 minutes / Cook Time: 0 minutes / Serve: 2

Ingredients:

- 1 tablespoon dried lavender buds
- 1 tablespoon dried lemon balm leaves
- 2 cups boiling water
- Honey or agave syrup (optional)
- Ice cubes
- Fresh lavender sprigs for garnish (optional)

Instructions:

1. Place the dried lavender buds and dried lemon balm leaves in a heatproof pitcher.
2. Pour boiling water over the herbs to steep.
3. Let the mixture steep for about 5 minutes to infuse the flavors.
4. After steeping, strain the elixir to remove the herbs, then let it cool to room temperature.
5. Once cooled, refrigerate the elixir until chilled.
6. When ready to serve, fill glasses with ice cubes.
7. Pour the chilled lavender-lemon balm elixir into the glasses.
8. Sweeten the elixir with honey or agave syrup if desired, stirring to combine.
9. Garnish each glass with a fresh lavender sprig, if available.
10. Stir well before sipping to distribute the flavors evenly. Enjoy the soothing and aromatic essence of this herbal elixir!

44. Raspberry-Rosemary Water

Prep Time: 5 minutes / Cook Time: 0 minutes / Serve: 2

Ingredients:

- 1 cup fresh raspberries
- 2 sprigs fresh rosemary
- 2 cups water
- Honey or agave syrup (optional)
- Ice cubes
- Fresh raspberries and rosemary sprigs for garnish (optional)

Instructions:

1. Rinse the fresh raspberries under cold water and drain them.
2. In a pitcher, combine the raspberries and fresh rosemary sprigs.
3. Pour water into the pitcher.
4. Let the mixture sit for about 10-15 minutes to allow the flavors to infuse.
5. After infusing, remove the rosemary sprigs and discard them.
6. If desired, sweeten the raspberry-rosemary water with honey or agave syrup, stirring until dissolved.
7. Fill glasses with ice cubes.
8. Pour the flavored water into the glasses.
9. Garnish each glass with a few fresh raspberries and a sprig of rosemary, if desired.
10. Stir well before sipping to enjoy the subtle sweetness and herbal essence of this infused water.

45. Orange-Clove Elixir

Prep Time: 5 minutes / Cook Time: 0 minutes / Serve: 2

Ingredients:

- 2 oranges, peeled and segmented
- 4 whole cloves
- 2 cups water
- Honey or maple syrup (optional)
- Ice cubes
- Orange slices and whole cloves for garnish (optional)

Instructions:

1. Peel the oranges and separate them into segments.
2. In a pitcher, combine the orange segments and whole cloves.
3. Pour water into the pitcher.
4. Allow the mixture to sit for about 10-15 minutes to infuse the flavors.
5. After infusing, remove the whole cloves from the pitcher.
6. If desired, sweeten the orange-clove elixir with honey or maple syrup, stirring until dissolved.
7. Fill glasses with ice cubes.
8. Pour the infused elixir into the glasses.
9. Garnish each glass with an orange slice and a whole clove, if desired.
10. Stir well before sipping to enjoy the warm and fragrant essence of this citrus-spiced elixir.

46. Cranberry-Cinnamon Infusion

Prep Time: 5 minutes / Cook Time: 0 minutes / Serve: 2

Ingredients:

- 1 cup fresh cranberries
- 1 cinnamon stick
- 2 cups water
- Honey or agave syrup (optional)
- Ice cubes
- Fresh cranberries and cinnamon sticks for garnish (optional)

Instructions:

1. Rinse the fresh cranberries under cold water and drain them.
2. In a pitcher, combine the cranberries and a cinnamon stick.
3. Pour water into the pitcher.
4. Allow the mixture to sit for about 10-15 minutes to infuse the flavors.
5. After infusing, remove the cinnamon stick from the pitcher.
6. If desired, sweeten the cranberry-cinnamon infusion with honey or agave syrup, stirring until dissolved.
7. Fill glasses with ice cubes.
8. Pour the flavored infusion into the glasses.
9. Garnish each glass with a few fresh cranberries and a cinnamon stick, if desired.
10. Stir well before sipping to enjoy the tartness of cranberries with a hint of warming cinnamon.

47. Spinach-Cucumber Detox Blend

Prep Time: 10 minutes / Cook Time: 20 minutes / Serve: 2

Ingredients:

- 2 cups fresh spinach leaves
- 1 cucumber, peeled and chopped
- 1 green apple, cored and chopped
- 1 lemon, peeled and seeded
- 1-inch piece of ginger, peeled
- 1/2 cup water

Instructions:

1. Place the spinach leaves, chopped cucumber, green apple, peeled lemon, and peeled ginger in the top compartment of the steam juicer.
2. Fill the bottom compartment of the steam juicer with water according to the manufacturer's instructions.
3. Assemble the steam juicer and turn on the heat. Steam the vegetables and fruits for about 15-20 minutes until they are soft and tender.
4. Once steamed, carefully remove the top basket from the steam juicer and let the contents cool slightly.
5. Transfer the steamed spinach, cucumber, apple, lemon, and ginger to a blender.
6. Add 1/2 cup of water to the blender and blend until smooth.
7. Strain the mixture through a fine-mesh sieve or cheesecloth to remove any pulp.
8. Serve the spinach-cucumber detox blend immediately over ice, if desired. Enjoy the refreshing and nutritious green juice!

48. Kale-Tomato Revitalizer

Prep Time: 15 minutes / Cook Time: 25 minutes / Serve:2

Ingredients:

- 2 cups kale leaves, stems removed
- 2 ripe tomatoes, chopped
- 1 celery stalk, chopped
- 1/2 red bell pepper, chopped
- 1/4 red onion, chopped
- 1 clove garlic
- 1/4 teaspoon cayenne pepper (optional)
- 1/2 cup water

Instructions:

1. Place the kale leaves, chopped tomatoes, celery, red bell pepper, red onion, garlic clove, and cayenne pepper (if using) in the top compartment of the steam juicer.
2. Fill the bottom compartment of the steam juicer with water according to the manufacturer's instructions.
3. Assemble the steam juicer and turn on the heat. Steam the vegetables for about 20-25 minutes until they are soft.
4. Once steamed, carefully remove the top basket from the steam juicer and let the vegetables cool slightly.
5. Transfer the steamed kale, tomatoes, celery, bell pepper, onion, and garlic to a blender.
6. Add 1/2 cup of water to the blender and blend until smooth.
7. Strain the mixture through a fine-mesh sieve or cheesecloth to remove any pulp.
8. Serve the kale-tomato revitalizer chilled or over ice. Enjoy the vibrant and nutritious vegetable juice!

49. Beet-Spinach Vitality Booster

Prep Time: 10 minutes / Cook Time: 20 minutes / Serve:2

Ingredients:

- 1 medium beet, peeled and chopped
- 2 cups fresh spinach leaves
- 1 green apple, cored and chopped
- 1 cucumber, peeled and chopped
- 1 lemon, peeled and seeded
- 1-inch piece of ginger, peeled
- 1/2 cup water

Instructions:

1. Place the chopped beet, spinach leaves, green apple, cucumber, peeled lemon, and peeled ginger in the top compartment of the steam juicer.
2. Fill the bottom compartment of the steam juicer with water according to the manufacturer's instructions.
3. Assemble the steam juicer and turn on the heat. Steam the vegetables and fruits for about 15-20 minutes until they are soft.
4. Once steamed, carefully remove the top basket from the steam juicer and let the contents cool slightly.
5. Transfer the steamed beet, spinach, apple, cucumber, lemon, and ginger to a blender.
6. Add 1/2 cup of water to the blender and blend until smooth.
7. Strain the mixture through a fine-mesh sieve or cheesecloth to remove any pulp.
8. Serve the beet-spinach vitality booster immediately over ice, if desired. Enjoy the earthy yet refreshing flavors of this nutrient-packed juice!

50. Carrot-Broccoli Green Cleanse

Prep Time: 10 minutes / Cook Time: 20 minutes / Serve: 2

Ingredients:

- 2 large carrots, peeled and chopped
- 1 cup broccoli florets
- 1 green apple, cored and chopped
- 1/2 cucumber, peeled and chopped
- 1-inch piece of ginger, peeled
- 1 lemon, peeled and seeded
- 1/2 cup water

Instructions:

1. Place the chopped carrots, broccoli florets, green apple, cucumber, peeled ginger, and peeled lemon in the top compartment of the steam juicer.
2. Fill the bottom compartment of the steam juicer with water according to the manufacturer's instructions.
3. Assemble the steam juicer and turn on the heat. Steam the vegetables and fruits for about 15-20 minutes until they are soft.
4. Once steamed, carefully remove the top basket from the steam juicer and let the contents cool slightly.
5. Transfer the steamed carrots, broccoli, apple, cucumber, ginger, and lemon to a blender.
6. Add 1/2 cup of water to the blender and blend until smooth.
7. Strain the mixture through a fine-mesh sieve or cheesecloth to remove any pulp.
8. Serve the carrot-broccoli green cleanse immediately over ice, if desired. Enjoy the vibrant and detoxifying qualities of this green juice!

51. Spinach-Pepper Antioxidant Blast

Prep Time: 10 minutes / Cook Time: 20 minutes / Serve: 2

Ingredients:

- 2 cups fresh spinach leaves
- 1 yellow bell pepper, chopped
- 1 red bell pepper, chopped
- 1 cucumber, peeled and chopped
- 1 green apple, cored and chopped
- 1 lemon, peeled and seeded
- 1-inch piece of ginger, peeled
- 1/2 cup water

Instructions:

1. Place the fresh spinach leaves, chopped yellow bell pepper, chopped red bell pepper, cucumber, green apple, peeled lemon, and peeled ginger in the top compartment of the steam juicer.
2. Fill the bottom compartment of the steam juicer with water according to the manufacturer's instructions.
3. Assemble the steam juicer and turn on the heat. Steam the vegetables and fruits for about 15-20 minutes until they are soft.
4. Once steamed, carefully remove the top basket from the steam juicer and allow the contents to cool slightly.
5. Transfer the steamed spinach, bell peppers, cucumber, apple, lemon, and ginger to a blender.
6. Add 1/2 cup of water to the blender and blend until smooth.
7. Strain the mixture through a fine-mesh sieve or cheesecloth to remove any pulp.
8. Serve the spinach-pepper antioxidant blast immediately over ice, if desired. Enjoy the refreshing and nutrient-packed green juice!

52. Tomato-Bell Pepper Garden Medley

Prep Time: 10 minutes / Cook Time: 20 minutes / Serve: 2

Ingredients:
- 2 large tomatoes, chopped
- 1 red bell pepper, chopped
- 1 yellow bell pepper, chopped
- 1 cucumber, peeled and chopped
- 1 celery stalk, chopped
- 1/4 red onion, chopped
- 1 clove garlic
- 1/4 cup fresh basil leaves
- 1/2 cup water

Instructions:
1. Place the chopped tomatoes, red bell pepper, yellow bell pepper, cucumber, celery, red onion, garlic clove, and fresh basil leaves in the top compartment of the steam juicer.
2. Fill the bottom compartment of the steam juicer with water according to the manufacturer's instructions.
3. Assemble the steam juicer and turn on the heat. Steam the vegetables for about 15-20 minutes until they are soft.
4. Once steamed, carefully remove the top basket from the steam juicer and let the vegetables cool slightly.
5. Transfer the steamed tomatoes, bell peppers, cucumber, celery, onion, garlic, and basil to a blender.
6. Add 1/2 cup of water to the blender and blend until smooth.
7. Strain the mixture through a fine-mesh sieve or cheesecloth to remove any pulp.
8. Serve the tomato-bell pepper garden medley chilled or over ice. Enjoy the garden-fresh flavors of this vibrant vegetable juice!

53. Spinach-Carrot Energizing Elixir

Prep Time: 10 minutes / Cook Time: 20 minutes / Serve: 2

Ingredients:
- 2 cups fresh spinach leaves
- 2 large carrots, peeled and chopped
- 1 green apple, cored and chopped
- 1 celery stalk, chopped
- 1-inch piece of ginger, peeled
- 1 lemon, peeled and seeded
- 1/2 cup water

Instructions:
1. Place the fresh spinach leaves, chopped carrots, green apple, celery, peeled ginger, and peeled lemon in the top compartment of the steam juicer.
2. Fill the bottom compartment of the steam juicer with water according to the manufacturer's instructions.
3. Assemble the steam juicer and turn on the heat. Steam the vegetables and fruits for about 15-20 minutes until they are soft.
4. Once steamed, carefully remove the top basket from the steam juicer and let the contents cool slightly.
5. Transfer the steamed spinach, carrots, apple, celery, ginger, and lemon to a blender.
6. Add 1/2 cup of water to the blender and blend until smooth.
7. Strain the mixture through a fine-mesh sieve or cheesecloth to remove any pulp.
8. Serve the spinach-carrot energizing elixir immediately over ice, if desired. Enjoy the invigorating and nutrient-rich elixir!

54. Broccoli-Cauliflower Green Fusion

Prep Time: 10 minutes / Cook Time: 20 minutes / Serve: 2

Ingredients:

- 1 cup broccoli florets
- 1 cup cauliflower florets
- 2 cups fresh spinach leaves
- 1 green apple, cored and chopped
- 1 cucumber, peeled and chopped
- 1 lemon, peeled and seeded
- 1-inch piece of ginger, peeled
- 1/2 cup water

Instructions:

1. Place the broccoli florets, cauliflower florets, fresh spinach leaves, chopped apple, peeled cucumber, peeled lemon, and peeled ginger in the top compartment of the steam juicer.
2. Fill the bottom compartment of the steam juicer with water according to the manufacturer's instructions.
3. Assemble the steam juicer and turn on the heat. Steam the vegetables and fruits for about 15-20 minutes until they are soft.
4. Once steamed, carefully remove the top basket from the steam juicer and allow the contents to cool slightly.
5. Transfer the steamed broccoli, cauliflower, spinach, apple, cucumber, lemon, and ginger to a blender.
6. Add 1/2 cup of water to the blender and blend until smooth.
7. Strain the mixture through a fine-mesh sieve or cheesecloth to remove any pulp.
8. Serve the broccoli-cauliflower green fusion immediately over ice, if desired. Enjoy the harmonious blend of green vegetables in this nutritious juice!

FRUIT CONCENTRATES

55. Concentrated Apple Syrup

Prep Time: 10 minutes / Cook Time: 40 minutes / Serve: 2 cups

Ingredients:

- 8 medium-sized apples, cored and sliced
- Water

Instructions:

1. Place the sliced apples into the top compartment of the steam juicer.
2. Fill the bottom compartment of the steam juicer with water according to the manufacturer's instructions.
3. Assemble the steam juicer and turn on the heat. Allow the apples to steam for about 40 minutes until they become soft and mushy.
4. Once steamed, carefully remove the top basket from the steam juicer and let the apples cool slightly.
5. Transfer the steamed apples to a large saucepan and mash them using a potato masher or fork to release the juice.
6. Bring the mashed apples to a gentle boil over medium heat. Then reduce the heat to low and simmer for about 20-30 minutes, stirring occasionally, until the liquid reduces and thickens to a syrup-like consistency.
7. Remove the saucepan from the heat and let the concentrated apple syrup cool completely.
8. Once cooled, strain the syrup through a fine-mesh sieve or cheesecloth to remove any pulp and solids.
9. Transfer the strained syrup to a clean, sterilized glass jar or bottle for storage.
10. Store the concentrated apple syrup in the refrigerator for up to 2 weeks. Enjoy drizzling over pancakes, waffles, yogurt, or using as a natural sweetener in various recipes!

56. Rich Concord Grape Concentrate

Prep Time: 15 minutes / Cook Time: 45 minutes / Serve: 2 cups

Ingredients:

- 4 cups Concord grapes, stems removed
- Water

Instructions:

1. Place the Concord grapes into the top compartment of the steam juicer.
2. Fill the bottom compartment of the steam juicer with water as per the manufacturer's instructions.
3. Assemble the steam juicer and turn on the heat. Allow the grapes to steam for about 45 minutes until they become soft and juicy.
4. Once steamed, carefully remove the top basket from the steam juicer and let the grapes cool slightly.
5. Transfer the steamed grapes to a fine-mesh sieve set over a bowl.
6. Press down on the grapes with the back of a spoon or a potato masher to extract as much juice as possible.
7. Transfer the extracted grape juice to a large saucepan and bring it to a boil over medium-high heat.
8. Once boiling, reduce the heat to low and simmer the grape juice for about 30-40 minutes, stirring occasionally, until it reduces to a thick and syrupy consistency.
9. Remove the saucepan from the heat and let the grape concentrate cool completely.
10. Once cooled, transfer the grape concentrate to a clean, sterilized glass jar or bottle for storage.
11. Store the rich Concord grape concentrate in the refrigerator for up to 2 weeks. Enjoy mixing with water or sparkling water for a refreshing grape drink, or use it as a natural sweetener in cocktails and desserts!

57. Mixed Berry Elixir

Prep Time: 10 minutes / Cook Time: 30 minutes / Serve: 2 cups

Ingredients:

- 1 cup fresh strawberries, hulled and halved
- 1 cup fresh blueberries
- 1 cup fresh raspberries
- Water

Instructions:

1. Place the strawberries, blueberries, and raspberries into the top compartment of the steam juicer.
2. Fill the bottom compartment of the steam juicer with water according to the manufacturer's instructions.
3. Assemble the steam juicer and turn on the heat. Allow the berries to steam for about 30 minutes until they become soft and juicy.
4. Once steamed, carefully remove the top basket from the steam juicer and let the berries cool slightly.
5. Transfer the steamed berries to a fine-mesh sieve set over a bowl.
6. Press down on the berries with the back of a spoon or a potato masher to extract as much juice as possible.
7. Transfer the extracted berry juice to a large saucepan and bring it to a boil over medium-high heat.
8. Once boiling, reduce the heat to low and simmer the berry juice for about 20-25 minutes, stirring occasionally, until it thickens to a syrup-like consistency.
9. Remove the saucepan from the heat and let the mixed berry elixir cool completely.
10. Once cooled, transfer the mixed berry elixir to a clean, sterilized glass jar or bottle for storage.
11. Store the elixir in the refrigerator for up to 2 weeks. Enjoy drizzling over desserts, mixing with yogurt or oatmeal, or using as a flavorful topping for pancakes and ice cream!

58. Tangy Citrus Burst Concentrate

Prep Time: 10 minutes / Cook Time: 40 minutes / Serve: 1½ cups

Ingredients:

- 2 large lemons, zest and juice
- 2 large oranges, zest and juice
- 1 grapefruit, zest and juice
- Water

Instructions:

1. Using a zester or a fine grater, zest the lemons, oranges, and grapefruit, being careful to avoid the bitter white pith.
2. Place the citrus zest and juice into the top compartment of the steam juicer.
3. Fill the bottom compartment of the steam juicer with water according to the manufacturer's instructions.
4. Assemble the steam juicer and turn on the heat. Allow the citrus fruits to steam for about 40 minutes until they release their juices.
5. Once steamed, carefully remove the top basket from the steam juicer and let the citrus mixture cool slightly.
6. Transfer the steamed citrus juice and zest to a large saucepan.
7. Bring the citrus juice to a boil over medium-high heat, then reduce the heat to low and simmer for about 30-35 minutes, stirring occasionally, until it thickens to a syrupy consistency.
8. Remove the saucepan from the heat and let the tangy citrus burst concentrate cool completely.
9. Once cooled, transfer the concentrate to a clean, sterilized glass jar or bottle for storage.
10. Store the tangy citrus burst concentrate in the refrigerator for up to 2 weeks. Enjoy using it as a flavoring for beverages, salad dressings, marinades, or desserts!

59. Fig and Date Infused Syrup

Prep Time: 15 minutes / Cook Time: 45 minutes / Serve: 1½ cups

Ingredients:

- 1 cup dried figs, stems removed and chopped
- 1 cup pitted dates, chopped
- Water

Instructions:

1. Place the chopped dried figs and dates into the top compartment of the steam juicer.
2. Fill the bottom compartment of the steam juicer with water as per the manufacturer's instructions.
3. Assemble the steam juicer and turn on the heat. Allow the figs and dates to steam for about 45 minutes until they become soft and tender.
4. Once steamed, carefully remove the top basket from the steam juicer and let the figs and dates cool slightly.
5. Transfer the steamed figs and dates to a large saucepan and mash them using a potato masher or fork.
6. Add enough water to the saucepan to cover the mashed figs and dates.
7. Bring the mixture to a gentle boil over medium heat, then reduce the heat to low and simmer for about 30-40 minutes, stirring occasionally, until the liquid reduces and thickens to a syrup-like consistency.
8. Once the syrup has thickened, remove the saucepan from the heat and let it cool slightly.
9. Strain the syrup through a fine-mesh sieve or cheesecloth to remove any remaining solids, extracting the infused syrup.
10. Transfer the strained syrup to a clean, sterilized glass jar or bottle for storage.
11. Allow the fig and date infused syrup to cool completely before sealing the jar or bottle.
12. Store the syrup in the refrigerator for up to 2 weeks. Enjoy drizzling over pancakes, waffles, yogurt, or using as a sweetener in coffee or tea!

60. Kiwi-Strawberry Concentrate

Prep Time: 10 minutes / Cook Time: 30 minutes / Serve: 2 cups

Ingredients:

- 4 ripe kiwis, peeled and sliced
- 1 cup fresh strawberries, hulled and halved
- Water

Instructions:

1. Place the sliced kiwis and strawberries into the top compartment of the steam juicer.
2. Fill the bottom compartment of the steam juicer with water according to the manufacturer's instructions.
3. Assemble the steam juicer and turn on the heat. Allow the kiwis and strawberries to steam for about 30 minutes until they become soft and juicy.
4. Once steamed, carefully remove the top basket from the steam juicer and let the fruits cool slightly.
5. Transfer the steamed kiwis and strawberries to a fine-mesh sieve set over a bowl.
6. Press down on the fruits with the back of a spoon or a potato masher to extract as much juice as possible.
7. Transfer the extracted fruit juice to a large saucepan and bring it to a gentle boil over medium-high heat.
8. Reduce the heat to low and simmer the fruit juice for about 20-25 minutes, stirring occasionally, until it thickens to a syrupy consistency.
9. Remove the saucepan from the heat and let the kiwi-strawberry concentrate cool slightly.
10. Once cooled, transfer the concentrate to a clean, sterilized glass jar or bottle for storage.
11. Store the kiwi-strawberry concentrate in the refrigerator for up to 2 weeks. Enjoy mixing with water or sparkling water for a refreshing beverage, or drizzling over desserts for added flavor!

61. Spiced Pear Nectar

Prep Time: 10 minutes / Cook Time: 40 minutes / Serve: 2 cups

Ingredients:

- 4 ripe pears, peeled and sliced
- 2 cinnamon sticks
- 4 cloves
- Water

Instructions:

1. Place the sliced pears, cinnamon sticks, and cloves into the top compartment of the steam juicer.
2. Fill the bottom compartment of the steam juicer with water according to the manufacturer's instructions.
3. Assemble the steam juicer and turn on the heat. Allow the pears and spices to steam for about 40 minutes until the pears are soft and tender.
4. Once steamed, carefully remove the top basket from the steam juicer and let the pears cool slightly.
5. Transfer the steamed pears to a blender or food processor and blend until smooth.
6. Strain the blended pear mixture through a fine-mesh sieve or cheesecloth to remove any pulp and solids, extracting pure juice.
7. Transfer the pear juice to a large saucepan and bring it to a gentle boil over medium-high heat.
8. Reduce the heat to low and simmer the pear juice for about 30-35 minutes, stirring occasionally, until it thickens slightly.
9. Remove the saucepan from the heat and let the spiced pear nectar cool slightly.
10. Once cooled, transfer the nectar to a clean, sterilized glass jar or bottle for storage.
11. Store the spiced pear nectar in the refrigerator for up to 2 weeks. Enjoy warming up with a comforting glass of spiced pear nectar on chilly days!

62. Plum Delight Concentrate

Prep Time: 10 minutes / Cook Time: 40 minutes / Serve: 2 cups

Ingredients:

- 6 ripe plums, pitted and sliced
- 1/4 cup honey or maple syrup (optional)
- Water

Instructions:

1. Place the sliced plums into the top compartment of the steam juicer.
2. If desired, drizzle the honey or maple syrup over the plums.
3. Fill the bottom compartment of the steam juicer with water according to the manufacturer's instructions.
4. Assemble the steam juicer and turn on the heat. Allow the plums to steam for about 40 minutes until they become soft and juicy.
5. Once steamed, carefully remove the top basket from the steam juicer and let the plums cool slightly.
6. Transfer the steamed plums to a blender or food processor and blend until smooth.
7. Strain the blended plum mixture through a fine-mesh sieve or cheesecloth to remove any pulp and solids, extracting pure juice.
8. Transfer the plum juice to a large saucepan and bring it to a gentle boil over medium-high heat.
9. Reduce the heat to low and simmer the plum juice for about 30-35 minutes, stirring occasionally, until it thickens to a syrupy consistency.
10. Remove the saucepan from the heat and let the plum delight concentrate cool slightly.
11. Once cooled, transfer the concentrate to a clean, sterilized glass jar or bottle for storage.
12. Store the plum delight concentrate in the refrigerator for up to 2 weeks. Enjoy drizzling over desserts, mixing with yogurt, or using as a natural sweetener in various recipes!

63. Apricot-Raspberry Essence

Prep Time: 10 minutes / Cook Time: 35 minutes / Serve: 1½ cups

Ingredients:

- 1 cup fresh apricots, pitted and sliced
- 1 cup fresh raspberries
- Water

Instructions:

1. Place the sliced apricots and raspberries into the top compartment of the steam juicer.
2. Fill the bottom compartment of the steam juicer with water according to the manufacturer's instructions.
3. Assemble the steam juicer and turn on the heat. Allow the apricots and raspberries to steam for about 35 minutes until they become soft and juicy.
4. Once steamed, carefully remove the top basket from the steam juicer and let the fruits cool slightly.
5. Transfer the steamed apricots and raspberries to a fine-mesh sieve set over a bowl.
6. Press down on the fruits with the back of a spoon or a potato masher to extract as much juice as possible.
7. Transfer the extracted fruit juice to a large saucepan and bring it to a gentle boil over medium-high heat.
8. Reduce the heat to low and simmer the fruit juice for about 25-30 minutes, stirring occasionally, until it thickens to a syrupy consistency.
9. Remove the saucepan from the heat and let the apricot-raspberry essence cool slightly.
10. Once cooled, transfer the essence to a clean, sterilized glass jar or bottle for storage.
11. Store the essence in the refrigerator for up to 2 weeks. Enjoy mixing with sparkling water for a refreshing beverage, drizzling over desserts, or using as a flavoring in yogurt or smoothies!

64. Guava-Pineapple Fusion

Prep Time: 10 minutes / Cook Time: 30 minutes / Serve: 2 cups

Ingredients:

- 2 ripe guavas, peeled and sliced
- 1 cup fresh pineapple chunks
- Water

Instructions:

1. Place the sliced guavas and pineapple chunks into the top compartment of the steam juicer.
2. Fill the bottom compartment of the steam juicer with water according to the manufacturer's instructions.
3. Assemble the steam juicer and turn on the heat. Allow the guavas and pineapple to steam for about 30 minutes until they become soft and juicy.
4. Once steamed, carefully remove the top basket from the steam juicer and let the fruits cool slightly.
5. Transfer the steamed guavas and pineapple to a blender or food processor and blend until smooth.
6. Strain the blended fruit mixture through a fine-mesh sieve or cheesecloth to remove any pulp and solids, extracting pure juice.
7. Transfer the guava-pineapple fusion juice to a large saucepan and bring it to a gentle boil over medium-high heat.
8. Reduce the heat to low and simmer the juice for about 20-25 minutes, stirring occasionally, until it thickens slightly.
9. Remove the saucepan from the heat and let the fusion juice cool slightly.
10. Once cooled, transfer the juice to a clean, sterilized glass jar or bottle for storage.
11. Store the guava-pineapple fusion in the refrigerator for up to 2 weeks. Enjoy sipping on this tropical delight or using it as a mixer for cocktails!

65. Mango-Coconut Dream

Prep Time: 10 minutes / Cook Time: 20 minutes / Serve: 2

Ingredients:

- 2 ripe mangoes, peeled and chopped
- 1/2 cup shredded coconut
- 1/2 cup pineapple chunks
- 1 banana, peeled
- 1/2 cup water

Instructions:

1. Place the chopped mangoes, shredded coconut, pineapple chunks, and banana in the top compartment of the steam juicer.
2. Fill the bottom compartment of the steam juicer with water according to the manufacturer's instructions.
3. Assemble the steam juicer and turn on the heat. Steam the fruits for about 15-20 minutes until they are soft.
4. Once steamed, carefully remove the top basket from the steam juicer and let the fruits cool slightly.
5. Transfer the steamed mangoes, coconut, pineapple, and banana to a blender.
6. Add 1/2 cup of water to the blender and blend until smooth.
7. Strain the mixture through a fine-mesh sieve or cheesecloth to remove any pulp.
8. Serve the mango-coconut dream immediately over ice, if desired. Enjoy the tropical flavors of this creamy and refreshing juice!

Made in United States
Troutdale, OR
11/24/2024

25235236R00022